Jamir and Chase's Great Adventure

Written By: Jennifer L. Baldwin

Jamir woke up one sunny morning with a big smile on his face. Today was a special day because he and his dog, Chase, were going to explore their new town for the very first time.

"Are you ready, Chase?" Jamir asked as he put on his shoes. Chase wagged his tail excitedly and barked, "Woof!" which meant, Yes, I'm ready!"

Jamir and Chase stepped out of their house and into the bright, cheerful neighborhood. The streets were lined with colorful houses, and friendly faces waved hello as they walked by.

Their first stop was the town park. Jamir loved the big, green trees and the playground filled with happy kids. Chase loved the open space where he could run and play fetch.

At the playground, Jamir met a boy named Liam. "Hi, I'm Jamir, and this is Chase," he introduced himself. Liam smiled and said, "Nice to meet you! Do you want to play with us?"

Jamir and Chase played with Liam and his friends, swinging on the swings and sliding down the slides. Chase chased a ball, his favorite game, and made everyone laugh with his funny antics.

After the park, Jamir and Chase continued their adventure to the town's farmer's market. The air was filled with delicious smells of fresh fruits, vegetables, and baked goods.

Jamir bought a juicy apple for himself and a tasty dog treat for Chase. They sat on a bench, enjoying their snacks and watching the busy market life around them.

Next, they visited the town library. Jamir loved reading books, and the library was filled with so many exciting stories. Chase quietly sat beside him, enjoying the peaceful atmosphere.

A kind librarian named Mrs. Green showed Jamir the children's section. "You can borrow any book you like," she said with a warm smile. Jamir picked a book about dogs, of course!

On their way home, Jamir and Chase discovered a small pet shop. Inside, they found all sorts of toys and treats for pets. The shop owner gave Chase a squeaky toy as a welcome gift.

As the sun began to set, Jamir and Chase walked back home. They were tired but happy from their exciting day. "We had a great adventure, didn't we, Chase?" Jamir said. Chase barked in agreement.

That night, Jamir snuggled into bed with Chase by his side. He dreamed of all the new friends they had made and the fun places they had discovered. He couldn't wait for their next adventure in their new town.

Jamir and Chase's exploration showed them the wonders of their new home, filling their day with joy, friendship, and discovery. They learned that a new place can be full of exciting surprises and warm welcomes.

The end.

We extend our deepest gratitude to our family for their unwavering love, encouragement, and support throughout this journey. Your belief in our dream made the creation of this first children's book possible.

Jamir & Jennifer

Copyright © 2024 Jennifer L. Baldwin

All rights reserved. No part of this publication may be reproduced, distributed, or transmitted in any form or by any means without the prior written permission of the publisher, except in the case of brief quotations embodied in articles and reviews.

ISBN: 979-8-3304-1590-8
Cover Designed and Published by JR Publishing, 2024

www.ingramcontent.com/pod-product-compliance
Lightning Source LLC
LaVergne TN
LVHW071700060526
838201LV00037B/390